THE · VOYAGES · OF

COLUMBUS

By Ken Hills

Illustrated by Paul Wright and others

Random House  New York

Foreword

''On the third day of the month of August [1492] on a Friday, half an hour before sunrise, I set my course for the Canary Islands . . . which are in the Ocean Sea, from there to embark on a voyage that will last until I arrive in the Indies.''
So wrote Columbus, setting out on the voyage that would bring him not to the Indies, but to the New World. He added:
''I decided to write down everything I might do and see and experience on this voyage from day to day.''

And so he did. When the journey was over, and he had come back to Spain in triumph, Columbus presented his record to Isabella, Queen of Spain. The original has been lost, but a copy has survived. From that copy, from letters and dispatches from later voyages, and from the story of his life written by his son Ferdinand emerges a true tale of astonishing adventures and achievements. This tale also shows the human story of the extraordinary man who discovered a new world, but refused to believe it.

Editor: Catherine Bradley
Designer: Robert Wheeler
Cover design: Amy Mayone

Library of Congress Cataloging-in-Publication Data
Hills, Ken
    The Voyages of Columbus / by Ken Hills; illustrated by Paul Wright and others.
        p.   cm.
    Includes index.
    Summary: Portrays the life of Columbus and his four voyages of exploration to the New World.
    ISBN 0-679-82185-6 (trade) 0-679-92185-0 (lib. bdg.)
    1. Columbus, Christopher—Journeys—Juvenile literature. 2. America—Discovery and exploration—Spanish—Juvenile literature. 3. Explorers—America—Biography—Juvenile literature. 4. Explorers—Spain—Biography—Juvenile literature.
    [1. Columbus, Christopher. 2. Explorers. 3. America—Discovery and exploration—Spanish.] I. Wright, Paul (Paul Anthony), ill. II. Title.
    E118.H55   1991
    970.01'5—dc20   91-7580

Phototypeset by Southern Positives and Negatives (SPAN), Lingfield, Surrey
Printed in Hong Kong

Acknowledgments

The publishers wish to thank the following for supplying photographs for this book:
Page 6 Bodleian Library, MS Bodley 264, fol. 218; 8 MAS; 18 the Mansell Collection; 22 The British Museum; 23 The British Museum (top), The Ancient Art & Architecture Collection (bottom); 31 The Hulton-Deutsch Collection (top), A.G.E. Fotostock (bottom).

The publishers wish to thank the following artists for contributing to this book:
Page 3 Edward Mortelmans of John Martin & Artists Ltd; 4/5 Paul Wright of John Martin & Artists Ltd; 6 Peter Jones of John Martin & Artists Ltd; 7 Janos Marffy of Jillian Burgess Associates Ltd (top); Malcolm Swanston (bottom); 8/9 Hemesh Alles of Maggie Mundy Illustrators' Agency; Malcolm Swanston (inset); 10/11 Stephen Lings of Garden Studio (top); Malcolm Swanston (bottom left); Edward Mortelmans (bottom right); 11 Peter Jones; 12 Stephen Lings (top); Malcolm Swanston (bottom); 13 Peter Jones (top); Janos Marffy (bottom); 14 Edward Mortelmans (top and middle); Janos Marffy (bottom); 15 Paul Wright; Janos Marffy (inset); 16 Kevin Maddison (top); Paul Wright (bottom); 17 Kevin Maddison; 18 Hemesh Alles; 19 Hemesh Alles (top); Kevin Maddison (bottom); 20 Paul Wright; 21 Hemesh Alles (top); Peter Jones (bottom); 22 Kevin Maddison; 23 Kevin Maddison; 24 Paul Wright (top left); Edward Mortelmans (bottom); 25 Paul Wright; 26–27 Hemesh Alles (top); 26 Janos Marffy (bottom); 28–29 Malcolm Swanston; 30 Hemesh Alles (top); Peter Jones (bottom).

Contents

Young Christopher

Christopher Columbus was born in the port of Genoa, in Italy, in 1451. His father, Domenico Columbus, was a wool weaver. Christopher, the eldest son, joined his family's trade as a boy. He probably never went to school.

Genoa at that time was a rich and busy port, famous for its map- and chart-makers. Year round, the great harbor was crowded with all kinds of ships—galleys, carracks and caravels—loading and unloading their cargoes. Ships in those days took on boys as young as eleven or twelve, so Christopher probably grew up as much at sea as on dry land. On voyages around the Mediterranean he learned to steer and sail ships, to judge speed and distance at sea and to recognize signs of good and bad weather. While still in his teens, Christopher left weaving and took up life at sea.

In 1476, when he was about twenty-five years old, Columbus sailed as an ordinary seaman in a convoy of Genoese ships bound for England. An enemy fleet attacked the convoy off Portugal's Cape St. Vincent. Columbus's ship sank in the battle, and he was lucky to reach shore.

Local people helped Columbus reach Lisbon, Portugal's capital. There he joined his younger brother Bartholomew, who was a map- and chart-maker.

The Portuguese were the leading seafarers of the age. They built the finest ships and had ventured farther down the coast of Africa and out into the Atlantic Ocean than had the people of any other nation. Columbus had come to the best place in the world to learn about ships and the sea.

During the following years Columbus learned to read and write in Portuguese, Spanish and Latin. He studied mathematics in order to navigate ships by the stars. He also went on voyages to England and Ireland. In 1478 he captained a ship to the Madeira islands, off the northwest coast of Africa, where he married and settled with his wife, Felipa, and where their son, Diego, was born. Meanwhile, a great idea was forming in his mind. In 1484 he was ready to present a daring business plan to the King of Portugal.

▼ Christopher nearly died in the battle off Cape St. Vincent. Ships of the two fleets became locked together, and the crews fought fiercely hand to hand. Christopher's cargo, highly inflammable resin, caught fire. In moments the whole boat was ablaze, and all aboard leaped into the sea to escape the flames. Christopher had been wounded in the battle, but he was young and strong and a powerful swimmer. Resting on an oar in the water, he managed to reach the shore.

A Small World

▲ Marco Polo was only seventeen when he set out for China in 1271. The journey through the mountains and deserts of Asia took four years. The Chinese Emperor Kublai Khan made Marco Polo an official at his court, and Marco served him for seventeen years before returning to Venice in 1295. Marco wrote a famous account of his adventures and the wonders of the Great Khan's empire.

Every year Portuguese seamen ventured farther along the west coast of Africa, looking for a direct sea route around Africa to the rich kingdoms of the East. This region, from India and the Spice Islands to China and Japan, was known to Europeans of the time as "The Indies." From the Indies came the luxuries craved by wealthy people of Europe: spices, silks, precious gems and gold. But the way to the East lay through enemy territory. Muslim rulers, bitterly hostile to the Christians of Europe, commanded the routes and taxed the goods heavily. In Europe itself, the Italian city of Venice controlled the trade and had grown immensely rich from its profits.

Two hundred years before Columbus's time, the Venetian traveler Marco Polo lived at the court of Kublai Khan, Emperor of China. Marco Polo's stories inspired Columbus to plan his adventure—to find a shorter way to the East by sailing west around the world.

▼ Merchants and their ships at the time of Marco Polo, on the waterfront of Venice. Many grew rich through Eastern trade.

CHINA

N

In Columbus's time educated people agreed that the shape of the Earth was round, like a ball. The belief that the Earth was flat had died out many years before. Knowledge of the sizes and shapes of the lands and the seas, however, was vague and uncertain.

The generally accepted view was simple. There was one vast ocean called the Ocean Sea. In it floated one huge island made up of Europe, Africa and Asia joined together. In theory, it would be possible to sail westward around the world from Europe to Asia. No one had tried it, because it was believed the distance was far too great for ships of the time. That was why the Portuguese, the finest sailors of the age, were exploring the route around Africa. They believed it was the only certain way of getting to the Indies.

Columbus was sure he knew better. But he thought the world was smaller than it really is and that Asia stretched thousands of miles closer to Europe than it actually does. By his calculation Japan was less than 3,000 miles west of Europe; he figured that by sailing westward he would reach the Indies in just a few weeks. His calculations were wrong.

▲ Spices were so rare and expensive that people sometimes mentioned them in their wills. Most spices came from the Indies.

▼ This map shows what Columbus believed the world was like compared with the world as it actually is. Columbus's ideas were based on maps drawn by the Florentine scientist Toscanelli. He, in turn, took most of his ideas about the Indies and China from Marco Polo.

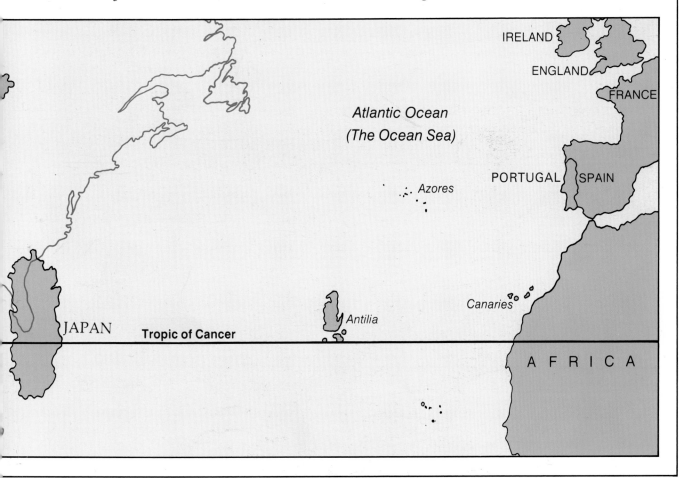

IRELAND
ENGLAND
FRANCE

Atlantic Ocean
(The Ocean Sea)

PORTUGAL SPAIN

Azores

Canaries

JAPAN **Tropic of Cancer** Antilia

A F R I C A

Selling a Dream

Columbus set out his ideas in a proposition called The Enterprise of the Indies. In 1484 he presented it to King John of Portugal. The king passed it on to a committee of learned men who poured scorn on the proposal. They declared that the Earth was far larger than Columbus claimed and that the distance to Japan—or *Cipangu*, as it was then called—was greater than any fleet could possibly sail. Bitterly disappointed, Columbus left Portugal for Spain in 1485. As his wife Felipa had died, he took with him his young son Diego.

In May 1486 Columbus offered his proposal to the royal court of Spain in Córdoba. Queen Isabella received him kindly but, as before, the Enterprise was placed before a committee of experts. The committee members could not agree, and years passed. The plan was rejected by England and France, and again by the King of Portugal. In 1490 the Spanish committee advised rejecting the Enterprise, but Columbus continued to present his ideas, and in January 1492 the queen finally agreed to support him. The Enterprise was accepted.

▲ Queen Isabella was only eighteen years old and King Ferdinand only nineteen when they married in 1469. They were a remarkable couple. Ferdinand was a ruthless and realistic politician. Isabella was a woman of great intelligence and wisdom.

Columbus left the Spanish court near Granada in despair after his plan had been turned down for the second time. But he got no further than the bridge at Pinos before messengers from the queen overtook him with orders to return. She had changed her mind, and his proposal for an expedition to the Indies had been accepted. One of her reasons was that Columbus intended to convert the people of the Indies to the Christian faith.

Getting Ready

For three more months Columbus argued with royal officials over details of the Enterprise, but in April 1492 the deal was signed. Columbus asked for a lot, and he got it. He was made commander of the expedition, and promised the title Admiral of the Ocean Sea. He, and his heirs after him, would become governor of any new lands he might claim for Spain, and he would receive ten percent of the profits from trading with them. If the Enterprise succeeded, Columbus would be a very rich man indeed – and a member of the Spanish nobility in the bargain.

Columbus set up his headquarters at Palos, a small port in southwest Spain. He hired three ships and took on ninety men and boys to sail them. The two smaller ships, the *Pinta* and the *Niña*, were caravels captained by two men from Palos, the brothers Martin and Vicente Pinzon. Columbus, as Admiral, sailed in the largest ship in the fleet, the *Santa María*, captained by Juan de la Cosa. The ships were tiny vessels in which to risk a voyage across a completely unknown ocean. The *Santa María*, 75 to 90 feet in length, was only about as long as a modern tennis court.

Isabella and Ferdinand gave Columbus a royal passport and letters of official greeting, one addressed to the Great Khan. By early August the little fleet was ready to sail.

First Voyage 1

At sunrise on Friday, August 3, 1492, the *Niña*, the *Pinta* and the *Santa María* left the harbor at Palos and headed south for the Canary Islands, 800 miles from Spain. The ships anchored there and loaded fresh stores for the voyage. On September 9 the fleet sailed due west, into the Ocean Sea.

For seven days steady winds blew the ships westward. On September 16 they came to vast, floating fields of fresh green weed. The men saw dolphins, and Columbus spotted a frigate bird, one that never rests on water. The excited crews took these signs to mean that land was near.

On September 19 Columbus revealed that the ships had come 400 leagues (about 1,400 miles) from the Canaries. His crew began to be afraid. The wind still blew west, and if it blew west forever, how could they sail back to Spain? On Saturday, September 22, the wind changed. Progress became slow and difficult, but the crew now had hope that they could return. Three days later, the wind turned and hurried the fleet westward again. At sunset on the twenty-fifth, the *Pinta*'s captain thought he could see land, but dawn showed that a low dark cloud in the dusk had deceived him.

The men had begun to plot against Columbus. They planned to pitch him overboard and return home. Seamen loyal to Columbus told him of the danger he was in, but he could do little about it. The fleet sailed on.

▲ Columbus knew that a frigate bird at sea meant land was near. Frigate birds never fly far from land because their feathers are not waterproof.

▼ The *Niña* was first rigged with triangular sails, for changeable Mediterranean winds. Columbus exchanged them for broad, rectangular sails, for steady winds expected in the Ocean Sea.

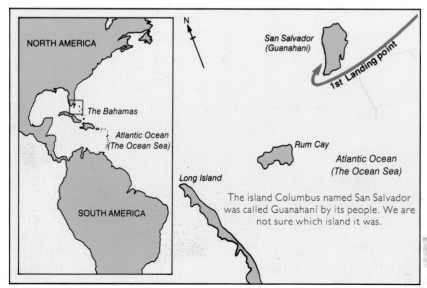

NORTH AMERICA

N

San Salvador (Guanahani)

1st Landing point

The Bahamas

Atlantic Ocean (The Ocean Sea)

Rum Cay

Atlantic Ocean (The Ocean Sea)

Long Island

SOUTH AMERICA

The island Columbus named San Salvador was called Guanahaní by its people. We are not sure which island it was.

The weather changed and the sea grew rough, but when fresh leaves and a carved stick were picked out of the water, the fears of the crews turned to excitement. At dusk, lights were seen in the distance, but they vanished, and the ships rushed on under a full moon.

At two A.M. the next morning, Friday, October 12, a lookout glimpsed a line of low cliffs in the moonlight. This time there was no mistake. The ships waited offshore until daybreak, and as the sun rose Columbus could see they had come to an island. He led the fleet around its southern tip and anchored in a small lagoon.

Fully armed, Columbus rowed ashore with his two captains, each carrying the green cross banner of the expedition, and a landing party. They knelt on the sand and kissed it, and they gave thanks to God. Columbus rose, unfurled the royal flag and took possession of the island for Spain in the name of King Ferdinand and Queen Isabella. He named it San Salvador (Holy Savior). As he spoke, naked people came out of the trees and down the beach.

▼ Columbus and his crew landed easily on Guanahaní, with no resistance from the native Arawaks. Columbus ordered his men to treat the Arawaks well. These fine intentions came to nothing. Fifty years after Columbus's landing, few of the native people were still alive. They died from European diseases or were worked to death as slaves on Spanish plantations and in gold mines.

First Voyage 2

Exploring the Indies

The Spaniards soon learned they had nothing to fear from the people of the island. They were friendly and respectful to Columbus's crews, believing them to be gods.

In the language of its people, the island was called Guanahaní. These people were Arawaks, but Columbus called them "Indians," for he was convinced that the island was part of the Indies. However, the Great Khan's city was clearly not on Guanahaní, so within three days of their first landing, all three ships set off to continue the search.

The fleet sailed over a sea scattered with fair, green islands, whose people were as friendly as those on Guanahaní. Some wore gold ornaments that they eagerly exchanged for the Spaniards' trinkets, explaining by hand movements that the gold came from a large rich island nearby. Columbus was overjoyed, certain that this island the Indians called "Colba" (now Cuba) was the island of Japan.

Cuba was a disappointment. The Indians were frightened of the Spaniards and ran away. The expedition found nothing of interest, and they sailed on.

▲ "Flocks of parrots darken the sun," wrote Columbus in his log. They made handsome gifts. He presented captive birds to the king and queen on his return.

▼ Using crude instruments, inaccurate charts and no landmarks of any kind, Columbus steered his ships with remarkable sureness over huge expanses of unknown ocean.

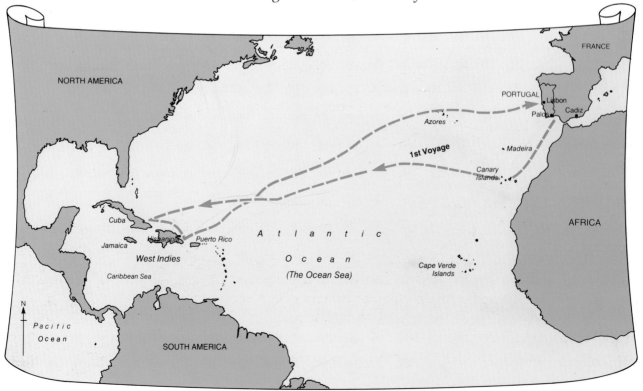

NORTH AMERICA

FRANCE

PORTUGAL
Lisbon
Palos
Cadiz

Azores

1st Voyage

Madeira

Canary
Islands

Cuba

Jamaica

Hispaniola Puerto Rico

West Indies

Caribbean Sea

A t l a n t i c

O c e a n

(The Ocean Sea)

Cape Verde
Islands

AFRICA

N

Pacific
Ocean

SOUTH AMERICA

Home in Triumph

The expedition arrived at another island, the most beautiful yet seen, on December 6. Columbus named it Hispaniola, in honor of Spain. The people were friendly. Gold seemed to be plentiful, for the Indians gave it readily to the visitors. They told Columbus that the gold came from islands not far away, so the expedition quickly put to sea again and sailed off to find them.

Columbus was now left with two ships, for the *Pinta* had slipped off to do some exploring on its own. Then, one night while Columbus and most of the crew slept, a ship's boy was allowed to steer the *Santa María*. The ship ran aground and stuck on a reef. The remaining caravel, the *Niña*, was too small to take both crews, so Columbus had a fort built ashore. He called it Navidad, and left thirty-nine of his men there. With the rest, he set sail for Spain.

At sea they found the *Pinta*, and the two ships went on together. They ran into violent storms, and not until March 15 did they come to Palos, where their voyage had begun.

Columbus was the hero of the hour. He had found a new route to the Indies just as he had said he would. He had even claimed rich new lands for Spain. Spaniards marveled at the golden ornaments and other wondrous things he had brought back from his travels. Word of his success spread through the countryside. His return was a triumph.

▲ The *Santa María* ran aground on Christmas morning, so Columbus called the fort he built from the ship's timbers "Navidad" (*Christmas* in Spanish). Thirty-nine men stayed behind in Navidad, well armed and with ample provisions. Columbus ordered them to treat the Indians kindly, but his words were ignored.

▼ Like Columbus, coconuts came to the Indies by sea, drifting on ocean currents. Sweet potatoes were new to the Spaniards. Columbus described them as "like carrots but tasting like chestnuts."

Ships and Sailing

▲ The one hot meal of the day was cooked on deck.

A Sailor's Life

Life for all but the rich was rough and comfortless in Columbus's time, but at sea there were added dangers of storm and shipwreck. On long voyages sailors risked death from hunger and thirst if provisions gave out. Thus, they prayed regularly to be kept safe from harm. Every day began with prayers.

A ship's crew was divided into two groups, or watches. The watches worked four hours and rested four hours, one after the other. Time on board was measured by a half-hour sandglass minded by a cabin boy. As the sand ran out, he turned the glass over and sang out the time of day.

The first duty of each watch was to pump the ship dry of any water that might have seeped in. After that, they cleared and cleaned the deck, set the sails, checked the cargo and kept the ship's gear in good order. Off duty, the crew slept where they could, in corners braced against the rolling of the ship. They had no privacy. Only the captain had private quarters.

Food on board was limited to what could be dried or preserved. Men fed on hard ship's biscuit, pickled or salted meat and fish, dried peas, cheese, honey, rice, nuts, olive oil and garlic. They drank wine or water. There was one hot meal a day, cooked over an open fire in a sandbox on deck. Hungry sailors ate meat that was tough, greasy and undercooked. Meals were collected in wooden bowls, cut with sheath knives, and eaten with the fingers.

▼ Sailors pulled on ropes to control the sails of the ship.

How Ships Were Sailed

Columbus often made mistakes in steering his ships by the sun and stars. He preferred to rely on a compass, a sandglass and pieces of wood. The most important instrument was the compass, which provided directions. The sandglass gave the time. Speed was worked out by dropping a piece of wood in the water at the bow and noting the time taken to pass it. Details of the ship's course were pegged out on a traverse board. It told an experienced seaman how far, how fast and in which direction the ship had traveled.

▲ Sailors used this diagram, based on a man's body, as a clock to tell the time by the stars at night.

Traverse board

The compass was used to set a ship's direction and keep it on course. The traverse board was a device for recording a ship's past track and how fast and far it had traveled.

Compass

The captain, or the officer of the watch, sailed the ship from a raised deck at the stern, which gave a good all-around view of the sea, the ship and the crew. The ship's compass was mounted before him. Directly below, on the main deck, stood the helmsman, who held the long wooden bar connected to the rudder. The officer shouted steering instructions to the helmsman through an open hatch in the deck at his feet.

Commanding a ship in uncharted waters in all weather was very hard work, even for someone as experienced as Columbus. Battling to keep the ship afloat and steady on the right course, he often spent days on end without sleep.

▲ Ships like these, called caravels, made up much of Columbus's fleet. They were small, sturdy ships, about seventy feet long and twenty feet wide. Since they could float in about seven feet of water, they could sail close to an uncharted coast.

Second Voyage 1

▲ The expedition banner bore a green cross between a crowned *F* and a crowned *Y* to mean King Ferdinand and Queen Isabella.

▼ The ships of Columbus's second voyage included the flagship *Mariagalante* and his favorite little *Niña*. Bright with banners, they put to sea from Cádiz to the sound of trumpets, harps, and the firing of cannons.

Soon after landing at Palos in March 1493, Columbus wrote to the king and queen. He reported that he had found the Indies and had claimed many islands for Spain. At Easter he received the royal reply. Ferdinand and Isabella addressed him as a nobleman, Don Christopher Columbus, and summoned him to attend their court "and make haste." Columbus set off in a triumphant procession across Spain, and people in towns and villages cheered him as he passed.

Columbus arrived at the court on April 20 and presented their majesties with evidence of his travels. He brought captive Indians, parrots, plants, fruits and spices, gold ornaments and samples of gold. The whole court then assembled in the royal chapel for a service of thanksgiving.

Within a month of arriving at court Columbus agreed to lead a second expedition. He was convinced that he had landed on islands just off Japan and the mainland of China. He was sure that not far beyond his first discoveries lay the wealthy cities and bustling harbors of the Great Khan's empire. The king and queen believed him, but others doubted. They maintained that the ''Indies'' Columbus had found were in the Ocean Sea halfway to the true Indies. No one yet realized that Columbus had discovered islands that fringed two unknown continents that stretched for 10,000 miles from north to south.

Preparations were quickly made. Seventeen vessels gathered in Cádiz harbor laden with plants, seeds, farm animals and tools. One ship would be broken up for wood to build the new settlement. The fleet carried over 1,200 men and boys, but no women. There were sailors, soldiers, ordinary colonists, officials, gentlemen and priests. The soldiers took weapons and ammunition, and horses and huge wolfhounds for hunting. On September 25, 1493, the expedition sailed from Cádiz, bound for the Indies.

▲ The cavalrymen on Columbus's second expedition brought their horses with them. These had to be tied up and supported, to stop them from running wild as the ship tossed and pitched.

The Discoveries

As he had done before, Admiral Columbus called first at the Canary Islands to take on fresh provisions. On October 12 the fleet set out again, taking a course well to the south of the first voyage. Sailing was smooth and quick, and on the twenty-second day, Sunday, November 3, the lookout on the flagship spied land ahead. The expedition had come to a new island, and Columbus named it Dominica (Spanish for Sunday). The fleet then set course to the north to find Hispaniola and the fort at Navidad.

The fleet sailed past chains of islands, which Columbus named as he went. On Guadeloupe, the Spaniards first saw signs of the ferocious Carib people, so greatly feared by the peaceful Arawaks. No Caribs were to be seen, but the landing party found half-eaten human limbs and baskets full of human bones. The Spaniards freed Arawaks who had been kept prisoners for future Carib feasts.

Late on November 27 the ships came to Navidad and anchored offshore until daylight. Flares were lit and cannons fired, but the shore remained dark and silent.

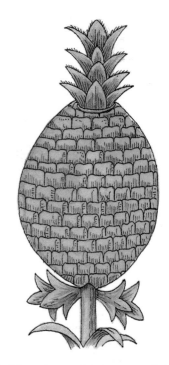

▲ The pineapple was one of the fruits discovered by Columbus on his voyages. This is a copy of an early picture of one.

Second Voyage 2

Disaster at Navidad

The next day an armed party landed at the fort. They found it smashed and burnt. Columbus learned from the local Indians that all thirty-nine men left at Navidad had been killed by natives from the center of Hispaniola. The Spaniards had been abusing and robbing the Indians until one tribe took revenge on the entire settlement.

Columbus took the fleet to search along the coast for a new site for the colony's capital. He sailed east, to be near the part of the island where he believed the Indians found gold. It was a difficult voyage. Both wind and currents were against the fleet, and after twenty-five days it had sailed only 30 miles. The crews were exhausted, and Columbus was a worried man. Back in Spain, he had promised quick profits and rich rewards, and so far he had produced neither. On January 2, 1494, he decided to anchor where there was some shelter from the wind; he sent men ashore to start building their future home. The settlement was named Isabela in honor of the queen.

In February Columbus sent the main fleet back to Spain, carrying a small cargo of spices, timber, a party of Indians and over 220 pounds of gold. For exploring, the Admiral kept behind the *Niña*, his flagship, and three other vessels.

▲ The men left behind at Navidad had behaved disgracefully. They had gone about the island seizing by force whatever took their fancy. Caonabò, chief of a tribe at the heart of the island, was determined to end it. He wiped out a Spanish raiding party, then destroyed the fort itself, with all its remaining defenders.

▶ This drawing shows how Europeans imagined the Caribs. This fierce tribe ate enemies killed in battle and took prisoners to eat later. The Spaniards called them *Caribales*, from which comes the English *cannibal*.

Conquest of Hispaniola

Before taking to the sea, Columbus set off with a well-armed party to explore the interior of the island. After crossing a range of mountains, they came to a broad, flat valley, so beautiful that Columbus named it the Vega Real (Royal Plain). Further on he left fifty men to build a small fort, and he then returned to Isabela. He found it in an uproar. It was an unhealthy spot, and many settlers had fallen sick. Several claimed that Columbus had lied about the gold to be found on Hispaniola. Mutiny was in the air, and Columbus was forced to put the worst troublemakers in irons. He then left to explore Cuba, leaving his brother Diego in command.

The voyage to Cuba and on to Jamaica was a disappointment, for the Admiral found neither gold nor the Great Khan. He returned to Isabela in September, where, to his great delight, his other brother Bartholomew awaited him. Soon another danger arose. Thousands of Indians were gathering in the Vega Real, threatening to drive the Spaniards into the sea. Columbus led an armed band against them, and after a short fight he utterly defeated them.

Columbus now learned that colonists who had returned to Spain had brought bad reports of his rule in Isabela. He decided to return to face his accusers and put his case to the king and queen. He left his brother Bartholomew in charge and arrived in Spain on June 11, 1496.

▲ A Spanish force of 200 on foot, twenty mounted soldiers and a pack of hunting dogs overcame several thousand armed Indians at the battle on the Vega Real. The Indians were terrified by the soldiers' horses and guns, which they had never seen before the Spaniards came.

▼ The Spaniards used dogs to hunt down and kill natives.

Third Voyage

In due course Ferdinand and Isabella summoned Columbus to their court. To the Admiral's relief, they appeared not to believe the bad reports about his rule of the colony in Hispaniola. The king and queen confirmed his titles and privileges, and appointed him to lead a third expedition to the Indies. But officials who were supposed to help get his fleet together delayed his plans whenever they could. Not until the last week of May 1498 did Columbus and his six ships sail for Hispaniola.

The expedition made good time to the Canary Islands, and there it split. Three ships sailed directly for Hispaniola, while the Admiral took the others farther south to cross the Ocean Sea. On July 13, the wind dropped. The ships lay motionless; they were in an area that came to be known as the doldrums. For eight days the crews sweltered under the tropical sun, fearing that they would die in that dreadful place. The wind at last blew them westward. On July 31, the dark shapes of three tall peaks appeared ahead. They were part of an island that Columbus named Trinidad. The fleet sailed on and anchored in a broad gulf between Trinidad and more land beyond, which Columbus took to be yet another island. As the ships lay there, a huge tidal wave bore down upon them. The water rose higher than the highest mast, but the ships escaped unharmed.

▼ The crews were terrified out of their wits by a tidal wave that struck the fleet while at anchor in the gulf. The sea piled up like a mountain, and with a monstrous roaring sound raced toward the ships. They rose to a great height and then fell almost to the seabed as the wave passed under them and ran on, foaming, out of sight.

Uprising in Hispaniola

The three ships sailed along the new shore, which Columbus claimed for Spain. He did not know that he had reached not an island, but the continent known today as South America.

Columbus now turned back to Hispaniola to rejoin his brothers. Bartholomew, in command of the colony, had given up the unhealthy settlement at Isabela and founded a new capital to the south which he called San Domingo. Columbus arrived there on August 31, 1498.

The colony was in a bad state. Food was short, and law and order had almost broken down. The colonists blamed the Columbus brothers, and word had gotten back to Spain. Much concerned, the king and queen sent their personal representative Francisco de Bobadilla to take charge in San Domingo. Bobadilla arrived in August 1500, to find Christopher and Bartholomew away and Diego, the third Columbus brother, in command. Bobadilla's first sight on landing was of seven Spanish bodies swinging from the town gallows. When Diego told him that five more were to be hanged the next day, Bobadilla released the prisoners and flung Diego in jail. As soon as Christopher and Bartholomew returned, they were put in chains and later, with Diego, shipped back to Spain.

▲ Bobadilla arrived to find two separate rebellions by colonists against Columbus's rule. Columbus himself was away hunting down rebels in the heart of the island.

▼ Columbus was now forty-seven years old, but he looked much older. He had arthritis, and he often fell ill.

Arawaks and Caribs

The Caribs and Arawaks both came from South America. The Arawaks were the first to arrive in the Caribbean and occupied most of the islands as far north as the Bahamas. By the time Columbus appeared, the Caribs had moved into the region. They had driven the Arawaks from many islands and had conquered what is now part of Puerto Rico.

Before Columbus, the Arawaks seem to have led a quiet, happy life. They were skilled farmers, and crops grew fast in the warm climate. They planted maize, cassava, sweet potatoes, groundnuts and French beans. Berries, wild fruits and fish were plentiful. They ate lizards and turtles for meat.

Dancing and singing, relaxing and smoking tobacco took up much of the Arawaks' time. They played a game with two teams on a marked field, in which each side tried to knock a ball over its opponent's goal line. The Arawaks made pottery and musical instruments. Their only metal was gold, which they used for ornaments. They were peaceful and unwarlike, and were terrified of the Caribs.

The Caribs were a ferocious people. They ate human flesh, for which they attacked other Caribs and Arawaks. They preferred the flesh of young men. Women were captured to have babies which were reared to be eaten at future feasts. At the age of four, boys were taken from their mothers and trained to become warriors. They fought with bows, firing arrows tipped with fish bones or turtle shell dipped in poison.

▲ This carved figure, called a zemi, was made for worship by the Arawaks. It represented the spirits which controlled natural forces, such as wind, rain and fire.

▲ The Arawaks rested and slept in *hamacas*—nets woven from cotton threads. In English, *hamaca* has become *hammock*. Sailors adopted them for sleeping on ship.

▼ Columbus praised the Indians' boats. He wrote, "They are made of tree trunks . . . forty or fifty men came in some of them, and they travel wonderfully fast."

Insulæ Canibalium

▲ A Venetian artist drew this picture of Caribs over a century after they first met the Spaniards. They had fierce courage and a strong warlike spirit. After the peaceable Arawaks, they were an unpleasant surprise for the Spaniards.

◄ An Arawak hut was about fifteen feet across. The roof was made of slender poles covered with leaves or grass. Doors were not needed, as the Arawaks did not steal.

▲ Arawaks smoked the dried leaves of a plant called *caoba*, using a pipe called a *tabaco*. The Spaniards misunderstood, and called the leaves *tabaco*.

Fourth Voyage 1

Ferdinand and Isabella had lost faith in Columbus, but they were shocked to learn he had been sent back to Spain in chains. They ordered his release and invited him to court. As always, they received him kindly, but they did not want him to govern their new lands. In September, Columbus learned to his bitter disappointment that he had been replaced as governor in Hispaniola by Don Nicholas de Ovando. In February, 1502, Ovando sailed with a splendid fleet of thirty ships and 2,500 sailors, soldiers and colonists.

Columbus was grieved, and his pride was hurt. He resolved to win back his good name by finding the way to the East. He applied to the court, and royal approval came quickly. On May 9 he sailed from Cádiz.

The fleet of four ships arrived off San Domingo on June 29. Columbus had been forbidden to land lest he stir up trouble, but he sent a message of warning to the new governor. He knew that a large treasure fleet was about to sail for Spain. From his experience of the Indies, he was sure that a hurricane was brewing, so he urged Ovando to keep the ships in the harbor until the storm had passed. Ovando scorned the advice, and the fleet put to sea. As it rounded the eastern tip of Hispaniola, the hurricane struck. Twenty-five ships went down; four managed to creep back to San Domingo, decks awash and sinking. Only one ship, the smallest in the fleet, got back to Spain.

▲ The four vessels of Columbus's fleet carried 140 people. Fifty-five were ships' boys aged between twelve and eighteen. Columbus's son, Ferdinand, aged thirteen, also came on the expedition.

◄ Ferdinand and Isabella gave Columbus their orders for his fourth voyage. They directed him to find a passage to the south of China, leading to the rich Spice Islands of the East.

► Many enemies of Columbus were lost when the treasure fleet went down. Among the 500 drowned was Francisco de Bobadilla, who had sent Columbus back to Spain in chains. The only ship that survived carried Columbus's personal share of the trade with the Indies. Columbus's enemies accused him of raising the storm by witchcraft. Columbus himself believed that it was a miracle.

Fourth Voyage 2

Thanks to Columbus's skill, his four ships were little damaged by the hurricane. On July 14 they began the search for the way to the East. After a fortnight, the expedition found a group of islands and a long coastline, with mountains beyond stretching from east to west. The Indians of this coast—part of present day Central America— were of a different race from the Arawaks and Caribs. The Spaniards exchanged goods with them and continued their search.

The months Columbus spent exploring this coast were the worst in his life. The fleet sailed back and forth, battling winds and currents. Rain fell for days without ceasing, and a waterspout once threatened to swamp the entire expedition. Worms attacked the planking of the ships so that they leaked badly. The fleet had to be drawn up on shore many times to repair the damage. Food on board went rotten, and the men took to having their meals after dark in order not to see what they were eating. They were exhausted and downcast, and Columbus himself lay sick for weeks on end.

On January 6, 1503, the ships anchored off the land Indians called Veragua (now part of modern Panama), where much gold was said to be found. A party sent to explore returned with gold scratched up with their hands. Encouraged, Columbus set up a trading post.

The men cleared land and built huts upon it, but local Indians, previously friendly, now turned against them. They attacked the trading post as the expedition was preparing to leave. The men pleaded not to be left behind; Columbus took them with him. While one of his ships was trapped in the river, the other three set sail for San Domingo.

▼ The Spaniards made huge profits in the Indies by exchanging inexpensive goods for pearls, jewels and gold.
The most popular trade goods were small brass bells. In Europe, these were fastened to the legs of birds used for hunting.

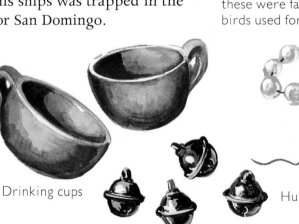

Sailors' caps

Drinking cups

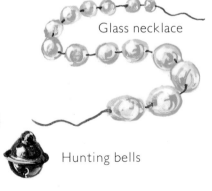

Glass necklace

Hunting bells

One caravel leaked so badly that it had to be abandoned. The two remaining ships, crowded with men, headed for San Domingo, but winds blew them off course to the coast of Cuba. Slowly the weary crews nursed their battered vessels against the wind toward Hispaniola. The waterlogged ships sank lower and lower in the water, until Columbus had to let the wind blow them south to the island of Jamaica. They arrived on June 25. The ships were useless; the crews built huts on the decks and waited for rescue.

Columbus sent two captains in Indian canoes to fetch help. They reached Hispaniola, but the governor, Ovando, did not hurry to Columbus's aid. Only in spring the next year was a ship sent for rescue.

On Jamaica half the men mutinied against Columbus. They stole Indian canoes and tried to sail away on their own, but the canoes sank in the surf and, sulkily, the mutineers came back. The local Indians began to refuse to supply food, and for a while the party went hungry. Rescue came in late June 1504 when a ship took the survivors back to San Domingo.

▲ After eight months the Indians grew tired of supplying food to the crews. Afraid his men would starve, Columbus tried a trick. From a calendar of the heavens, he knew that an eclipse of the moon was due. The Indians were sent for, and he warned them that God was about to punish them for refusing to supply food. He said God would give them a clear sign the following night. Next evening the Indians gathered at the ships, and the moon rose, blood red. As it climbed, it began to disappear. In terror, the Indians begged the Admiral to ask God to restore it. He retired to his cabin and returned as the moon began to reappear. There was no shortage of food after that.

Columbus's Four Voyages

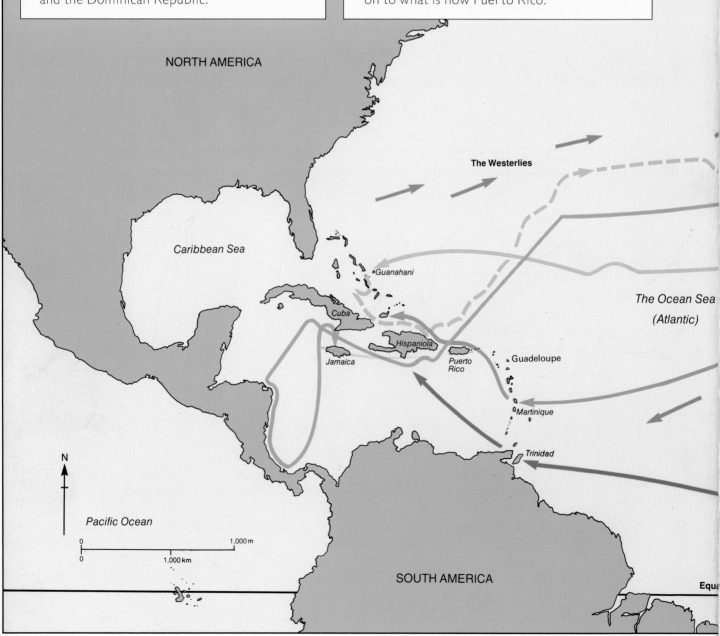

The First Voyage:
August 1492–March 1493

In 1492 any ship could have reached America from Europe by sailing west for long enough, but only Columbus dared to try. His other great achievement was to find Spain again. On the first voyage, Columbus discovered the islands now called the Bahamas, and went on to explore Cuba and "Hispaniola," now Haiti and the Dominican Republic.

The Second Voyage:
September 1493–June 1496

The Indians Columbus met on Hispaniola told him that many more islands lay to the south and west. Columbus took a more southerly course on his second voyage and, twenty-two days from the Canaries, he sighted the island he named Dominica. He turned north and west, sailed through the Lesser Antilles and on to what is now Puerto Rico.

NORTH AMERICA

The Westerlies

Caribbean Sea

Guanahani

The Ocean Sea
(Atlantic)

Cuba

Hispaniola

Jamaica

Puerto
Rico

Guadeloupe

Martinique

Trinidad

N

Pacific Ocean

0   1,000 m

0   1,000 km

SOUTH AMERICA

Equa

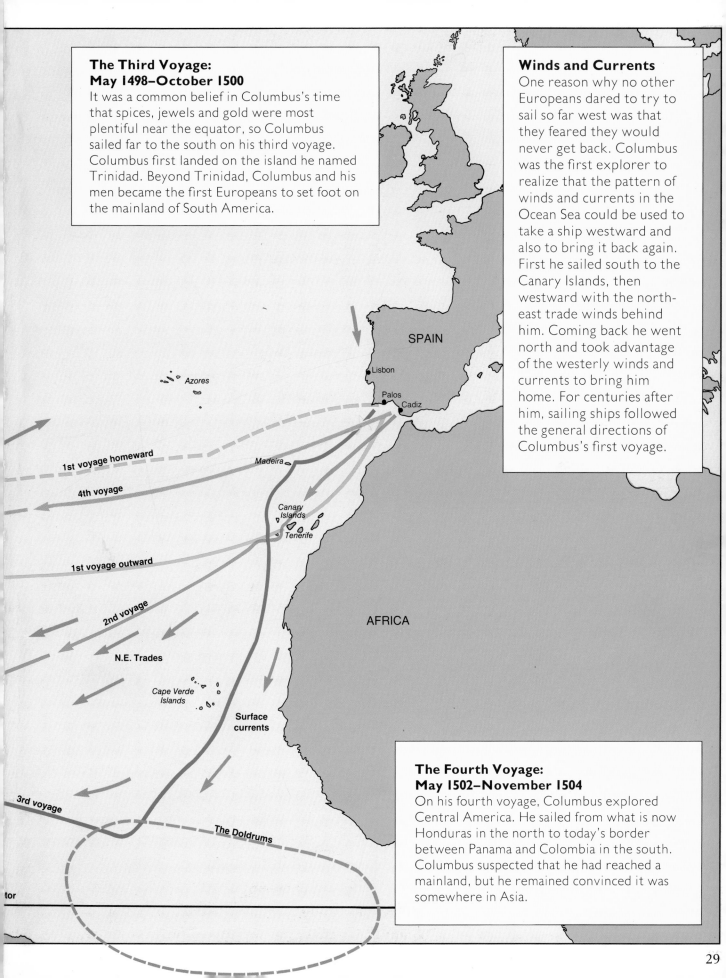

The Third Voyage:
May 1498–October 1500

It was a common belief in Columbus's time that spices, jewels and gold were most plentiful near the equator, so Columbus sailed far to the south on his third voyage. Columbus first landed on the island he named Trinidad. Beyond Trinidad, Columbus and his men became the first Europeans to set foot on the mainland of South America.

Winds and Currents

One reason why no other Europeans dared to try to sail so far west was that they feared they would never get back. Columbus was the first explorer to realize that the pattern of winds and currents in the Ocean Sea could be used to take a ship westward and also to bring it back again. First he sailed south to the Canary Islands, then westward with the north-east trade winds behind him. Coming back he went north and took advantage of the westerly winds and currents to bring him home. For centuries after him, sailing ships followed the general directions of Columbus's first voyage.

SPAIN

Azores

Lisbon

Palos

Cadiz

1st voyage homeward

4th voyage

Madeira

Canary Islands

Tenerife

1st voyage outward

2nd voyage

AFRICA

N.E. Trades

Cape Verde Islands

Surface currents

3rd voyage

The Doldrums

The Fourth Voyage:
May 1502–November 1504

On his fourth voyage, Columbus explored Central America. He sailed from what is now Honduras in the north to today's border between Panama and Colombia in the south. Columbus suspected that he had reached a mainland, but he remained convinced it was somewhere in Asia.

tor

Home to Spain

The Admiral hired a ship in San Domingo and returned to Spain with his brother Bartholomew and his young son Ferdinand. They arrived on November 7, 1504.

Columbus took a house in Seville and waited there for a call from Ferdinand and Isabella to attend them at court, but the summons never came. Queen Isabella was sick and on November 26 she died. Columbus was deeply distressed by her death, for Isabella had been his greatest friend and supporter at court and had many times shielded him from his enemies.

The Admiral was not a poor man. His share of the profits from the Indies made him rich, but he was not content. He made repeated complaints to the royal court that he had been cheated of his rewards, and he appealed to be restored as governor of the new lands in the Indies.

But Columbus's fame had faded. Few paid heed to the complaints of a sick and elderly mariner whose sailing days were done. In spring 1505 he was called to court. Ferdinand heard his petition courteously, but nothing followed. Columbus became quite ill and soon could not leave his bed. On May 20, 1506, in the company of relatives and friends, he died.

Our debt to Columbus

Up until the end of his life, Columbus thought the lands he had claimed were islands close to Asia. If he had claimed that the long coastline explored on his third and fourth voyages was part of a new world, perhaps it would now bear his name. As it was, the continent was named after a later explorer, Amerigo Vespucci.

The day of Columbus's first landing in the New World is celebrated throughout the Americas, although the continents were, of course, settled thousands of years earlier by the people Columbus called "Indians." Columbus was not even the first European to set foot in America. Viking explorers, and perhaps others, had been there before him.

But the voyages of Columbus opened the way to the New World and changed life forever on both sides of the Atlantic. No exploration in history has ever taught us more.

▲ The Italian traveler Amerigo Vespucci described what was considered the "discovery" of a new continent in a book published in 1507. He had made journeys to the coast of South America in 1499 and 1501.

▶ This map, drawn in 1532, shows the new name for the continent, "America," after Amerigo Vespucci. It was first used on a map in 1507, after the mapmaker had read Amerigo's book.

▲ The hardships and anxieties that Columbus suffered made him look older than he was. He lamented, "My body is sick and wasted."

▶ This statue in Spain shows Columbus as the visionary explorer he was in life. He points westward, toward the New World.

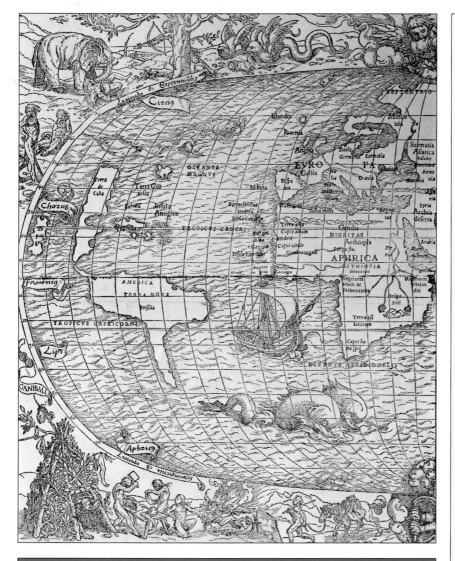

Chronology

1451 Columbus born in Genoa.

1476 He makes his home in Portugal.

1484 Portuguese turn down his Indies proposal.

1485 He goes to Spain.

1486 Presents proposal to Spaniards.

1492 Proposal accepted by Ferdinand and Isabella.
Aug 3 Columbus sails on his first voyage.
Oct 12 Lands on Guanahaní (Bahamas).
Dec 26 Founds Navidad.

1493 *Jan 4* Sails for Spain.
March 15 Arrives at Palos.
Sept 25 Columbus sails on his second voyage.
Nov 27 Finds Navidad destroyed.

1495 *Mar 28* Wins battle of the Vega Real.

1496 *Mar 10* Leaves for Spain.
June 11 Arrives at Cádiz.

1498 *May 30* Columbus begins third voyage.
July 31 Trinidad sighted.

1500 *End Oct* Arrives home in chains.

1502 *May 9* Columbus sails on the Fourth Voyage.
June 30 Hurricane. Treasure fleet goes down.

1503 *June 25* Stranded on Jamaica.

1504 *June 29* Columbus rescued.
Sept 12 Sails for home.
Nov 7 Lands in Spain.

1506 *May 20* Columbus dies.

Index